Treasury of

Baby Animal Stories

Cover illustrated by
Rose Mary Berlin

publications international, ltd.

Louis Weber, C.E.O.
Publications International, Ltd.
7373 North Cicero Avenue,
Lincolnwood, Illinois 60712

3rd Floor, 3 Princes Street
London WIR 7RA

www.pilbooks.com

8 7 6 5 4 3 2 1

ISBN: 0-7853-8224-0

Contents

Contents

Farm Puppy

Written by Lenaya Raack

Illustrated by Deborah Colvin Borgo

In a corner of the barn, four tiny puppies snuggle against Mother Dog's side. They are four days old. Mother Dog made a bed for them away from the clucking hens, away from the curious piglets, and away from the busy farmer.

The tiny puppies sleep most of the day. They cannot see, they cannot hear, and they cannot walk. The puppies need Mother Dog to take care of them.

Every day the puppies drink Mother Dog's milk, and Mother Dog gives her babies a bath. And every night Father Dog sleeps near them. During the day, he helps the farmer take care of his sheep.

The farmer watches one of the puppies explore the barn. His name is Farm Puppy, and he is three weeks old now. He can see and hear all the animals who live in the barn. He hears the rooster crow every morning. He sees the brown hen sitting on her eggs. He hears the piglets squealing as they play. And he sees the brown cow eating the hay.

Today, Farm Puppy visits the baby chicks. Farm Puppy wants to round up the chicks. He walks in a circle around the chicks, trying to move them to the back of the barn. When Farm Puppy comes too close, the chicks run and hide under Mother Hen's feathers. Mother Hen squawks at Farm Puppy, and he runs back to Mother Dog.

The bright sun shines on the barnyard. It is springtime! Farm Puppy is five weeks old. He likes to watch his mother and father herd the sheep. Father Dog herds the sheep through a gate. Mother Dog chases after a sheep that is running away. Soon Farm Puppy will be able to herd sheep, too. But for now, he practices with other barnyard animals.

Farm Puppy runs over to the chickens, but they keep eating. He races over to Mother Pig and her piglets. Mother Pig just snorts at Farm Puppy. She doesn't want anyone near her piglets. Farm Puppy runs over to the calves but they are eating, too. No one seems to listen to Farm Puppy.

Now Farm Puppy is six weeks old. He finally gets to help the farmer, Mother Dog, and Father Dog take the sheep to the pasture! Farm Puppy follows Mother and Father Dog as they move the sheep out of the farm gate. The farmer blows his whistle and moves his hands. When the farmer moves his hand, Father Dog walks around the sheep. When the farmer whistles, Mother Dog barks at the sheep and makes them move.

Now Farm Puppy plays follow the leader. When Mother Dog runs after a sheep, Farm Puppy runs after the sheep, too. When Father Dog lies down and stares at the sheep, so does Farm Puppy. This is good practice for being a sheepdog!

Farm Puppy has been exploring the pasture while the sheep eat. It is hot in the sun. Farm Puppy looks for some water to drink. In the corner of the pasture, he finds a pond. Farm Puppy bends his head to take a drink. Suddenly, he sees a strange dog in the water! Farm Puppy lies on the ground and stares. But the dog has gone away. Farm Puppy stands up again. He sees the dog again!

Then Farm Puppy barks at the strange dog. The other dog barks, too. Farm Puppy circles the pond. But the dog still stares back. Farm Puppy runs toward the dog and then—splash! Farm Puppy is all wet. The farmer rescues the puppy and takes him back to the herd.

Farm Puppy is staying home today. He likes to play in the barnyard. Farm Puppy walks up to the geese, and stares at them. He is trying to herd them into the barn. But the geese just stare back! When they walk away from the barn, Farm Puppy tries to stop them. He circles them and barks loudly.

Honk! Honk! The geese run in all different directions! Farm Puppy races after them, into the squawking chickens, over the hay bales, through the legs of the mooing calves, under the fence and back again. Then they fly on top of a hay wagon. Farm Puppy stops and barks. But they will not come down. And they will not go into the barn. Herding is hard work!

Suddenly Farm Puppy hears another kind of honk. The children have come home on the school bus! Farm Puppy races to meet them. The bus starts to move, but it is too fast for Farm Puppy to catch.

"Here, Puppy!" the children yell. Farm Puppy runs to them as they walk toward the house. But Farm Puppy doesn't want them to go into the house. He circles the children. The children stop.

"Puppy must think we are some kind of funny sheep," the boy says. When Farm Puppy sits and stares, the children start walking. When Farm Puppy stands and barks, they stop. Finally they tell Farm Puppy to sit and be a good dog.

Just then, Farm Puppy hears the farmer's whistle. The farmer is calling him! Farm Puppy is now six months old. The farmer must teach Farm Puppy to be a good sheepdog. They practice every day. Farm Puppy learns what to do when the farmer whistles and moves his hands.

Farm Puppy learns how to take the sheep out the gate and bring them back in again. Farm Puppy learns to move the sheep so that he is on one side of them and the farmer is on the other. The farmer teaches Farm Puppy what to do when a sheep runs away. Farm Puppy learns very fast. Soon Farm Puppy will be able to move the sheep like his mother and father.

Today, Farm Puppy and Father Dog are in the pasture with the sheep. The sky darkens as rain begins to fall. Thunder sounds, and the farmer decides it's time to take the sheep back to the farm.

The sheep are afraid. They start to run away. Farm Puppy circles the sheep like his father. The farmer signals. Now Farm Puppy and Father Dog must turn the sheep. The sheep head for the farm.

When the thunder roars again, one lamb runs away. Farm Puppy runs after it. Father Dog and the farmer take the sheep back to the farm. They wait for Farm Puppy to come home with the lamb.

Finally, the farmer and Father Dog go looking for them. There is no sign of Farm Puppy or the lamb. Father Dog barks. Then Farm Puppy barks back. The farmer and Father Dog run to Farm Puppy. They find Farm Puppy and the lamb. The lamb is stuck in mud. The farmer pulls him out. He pats Farm Puppy and tells him that he is the best sheepdog.

Baby Penguin

Written by Jennifer Boudart

Illustrated by Lori Nelson Field

Ark! Ark! At the frozen seaside, the penguins greet each other with a loud barking noise. Father Penguin returns from a swim in the sea. He builds up speed until he can leap out of the water and land on the ice. Then he shakes the water off his feathers. It is now Father Penguin's turn to stay close to the nest so Mother Penguin can go fishing.

Mother Penguin climbs from the nest. Her movements wake her baby. Baby Penguin blinks her bright black eyes.

Baby Penguin is a slowpoke. When she was born, she took half a day to break out of her shell. It takes a long time for her to eat, too. And even though she is three weeks old, she has never left her nest.

Baby Penguin looks around. Penguins are everywhere, and they are all squawking loudly! They sure are noisy.

Penguins are birds, but they cannot fly. Baby Penguin's wings are really more like flippers. Although she'll never fly in the sky like other birds, Baby Penguin will be able to fly through the water with her special wings.

Each family of penguins guards its nest. If a stranger gets too close, Father Penguin stretches his neck. His neck feathers fluff out. He points his head up to the sky and grunts. Baby Penguin stretches her neck and grunts, too.

Father Penguin and his baby tell the stranger to keep away from their home.

Father Penguin protected Baby Penguin when she was just an egg, too. He held the egg on top of his feet so it wouldn't touch the ice for almost two months. A flap of warm belly skin covered the egg and kept it warm. Baby Penguin is lucky to have Father Penguin!

Mother and Father Penguin must go fishing often to catch enough food for their tiny baby. They will have to leave her for a while. Baby Penguin's mother and father bring her to a group of young penguins. She slowly waddles after them.

Baby Penguin will be safe in this group. The older penguins will watch for danger. They circle around the babies and shelter them from cold winds.

If an enemy approaches the babies, the adult penguins will beat their wings and screech, scaring the enemy away.

Baby Penguin snuggles with the others. She falls asleep. Baby Penguin does not notice the group moving away from her. She wakes up and sees a bird diving at her!

Luckily, an older penguin is nearby. The big penguin runs toward Baby Penguin, waving his flippers and barking loudly. He scares the bird, and it flies away!

Baby Penguin hasn't learned how to escape danger, yet. Soon Mother and Father Penguin will teach her how to swim really fast through the water and away from danger.

Baby Penguin goes back to the other penguins. She is frightened and very hungry. Suddenly she hears her father calling to her! Will he find her? Baby Penguin is lost in a crowd of fuzzy little black penguins that look just like her.

Baby Penguin lifts her head and barks as loudly as she can. Her parents hear her over all the other noise. They find her!

Baby Penguin is happy to return to the nest with Mother and Father Penguin. She knows it is time for them to feed her the fish that they have caught in the sea.

Penguins get all of their food from the ocean. They eat fish, crab, and squid. They also eat small sea creatures called plankton. Penguins have spiky tongues that help them grip the slippery fish in their beaks.

When penguins get thirsty, they can eat snow to quench their thirst. And they can drink salty ocean water without getting sick.

After Baby Penguin eats her meal, Mother and Father Penguin "clean house." They replace the rocks that have tumbled off their nest pile.

A snowstorm has blown in from the ocean. Large, white flakes are falling everywhere. Baby Penguin is lucky to have her parents to shelter her from the cold winds and keep her warm.

Penguins have bodies that are built for the coldest weather on earth. Their bodies are covered with three layers of tiny, waterproof feathers, which keep out the cold wind and keep in their body heat. They also have a thick layer of fat all over their bodies to keep them warm.

The penguin family huddles together. When the sky clears, the snow will melt. It will be fishing time again!

A few weeks have passed. Baby Penguin has new feathers. Now she looks like a grown-up. Baby Penguin flaps her flippers. Now she is ready to go somewhere. So are the other penguins. They form a big group near the water.

Baby Penguin follows them. She uses her flippers to slide across the cold ice on her belly.

Baby Penguin quickly discovers that sliding is the best way to get around on the cold snow and ice. Penguins do this by using their fat bellies as toboggans.

It is now time for the young penguins' first swim in the sea. Baby Penguin is one of the last little penguins to dive in. She's really swimming fast! Baby Penguin is no longer such a slowpoke!

Little Honeybee

Written by Jennifer Boudart

Illustrated by Andrea Tachiera

The farmer's beehives sit in a field of tall, yellow sunflowers. The beehives do not look very fancy. They are made from stacks of wooden boxes. Each wooden box has a special bottom, like a screen, just perfect for a bee to build a home. An opening at the bottom of the hive is where the bees come and go.

This hive is home to thousands of honeybees. They live together in a colony. The honeybees make honey and beeswax that the farmer sells. They feed on flowers, trees, and vegetable fields on the farm. By feeding on the plants and carrying the plants' pollen from one flower to another, the honeybees help the plants to grow.

Honeybees start their lives as tiny eggs. In spring, the young bees begin to hatch. A honeybee does not have eyes, wings, or legs until it is at least two weeks old. At this stage it is called a larva. Until its body forms, the baby bee lives in a tiny, six-sided cell made from beeswax. These cells put together make honeycombs. The other bees in the hive must feed the baby bees while they live in these cells.

This baby bee is almost three weeks old. She is crawling out of her cell for the first time. To get out, she must eat a hole through one wall of her cell. It is hard work!

The newborn honeybee goes to work right away. She is born knowing what her job is in the hive. The little bee crawls in and out of empty cells. She makes sure they are clean. The queen bee will only lay eggs in clean cells. Young female bees like this bee are called workers. They take care of the hive and gather food. The queen bee is the only bee that lays eggs for the hive. And male bees help the queen to lay her eggs.

The little bee will not leave the hive for three weeks. During this time, she is a "house bee." She helps clean the hive. She feeds baby bees. And she builds new cells in the hive with beeswax.

Beeswax is like cement. The little bee makes the beeswax with her body. She carefully takes bits of beeswax from her belly and builds new cells. Some cells will hold baby bees. Others will store honey and food for the colony. When the bees have made enough honey, the farmer will take some honey from the hive. He will leave enough for the colony to eat.

The young honeybee is growing. She is almost ready to leave the hive. She has one last job as a house bee, though. It is a very important job. She must guard the entrance to the hive. Other animals, even other bees, will try to steal honey from the hive.

As she stands guard, a robber bee from another hive tries to sneak past the little bee to steal food. The little bee touches the robber bee, and right away she knows the bee is not from her colony. The little bee pushes the robber bee away from the hive, and the stranger flies away. The hive is safe again!

The little honeybee is ready to take her first flight! Now she is called a field bee. She will begin to collect food for the hive. When her wings move up and down very fast, they make a buzzing sound. Soon the little bee rises into the air. She circles around the hive many times to learn what her hive looks like so she can find her way back to it. Her next flight will be to the farmer's fields to find food.

The little honeybee buzzes through the summer air. She is looking for just the right flowers. She looks for flowers with bright colors and a sweet scent. Her special eyes help her find which flowers are filled with nectar. When the little bee finds a clover, she lands and sips the liquid nectar from the flower with her tongue.

The little honeybee will fill her tummy with sweet nectar and take it back to the hive. The nectar mixes with a special enzyme that bees have in their honey stomachs. This mixture is called honey. The honey is then stored in one of the beeswax cells that the little bee helped to make in the hive.

As the little bee collects nectar, she also gathers pollen from flowers. Pollen looks like yellow dust. The pollen sticks to the bee's furry legs. She brushes the pollen into little baskets on her back legs.

The bee visits many different flowers when she feeds. Some of the pollen that she has collected from one flower falls onto a new flower. When the pollen from one flower mixes with another, a seed will form. The seed makes a new plant. This is called pollination.

When the little bee's baskets are full, she takes her pollen back to the hive. The pollen will be stored for food.

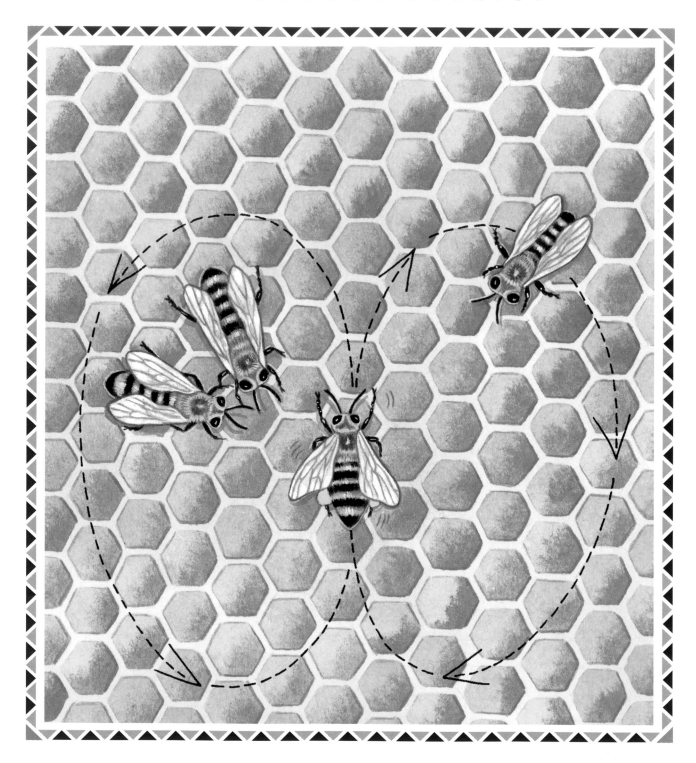

The little bee returns to her hive. She gives her load of nectar and pollen to a house bee.

The little bee flies farther into the hive so she can tell her brothers and sisters where she found the tasty food. She does a dance! The little bee turns in a circle and wiggles her body. These movements let the other bees know how far away the flowers are. The movements also tell the bees what direction to fly to find the food.

The little bee also gives off a smell that tells the other workers what kind of flowers she found.

It is time for the farmer to harvest, or collect, the honey from the hive. The farmer sprays smoke in the top box of the hive. The little bee does not like the smoke, so she crawls to the bottom of the hive with the other bees. This smoke also makes the bees move really slowly which means the farmer has less of a chance of getting stung after spraying the smoke.

The farmer lifts some honey-filled cells from the top box and removes the honey. She leaves enough honey for the colony to eat. She'll take the honey home where it will be processed, stored in a jar, and sold to customers.

After the farmer has harvested as much as she needs, the bees know the hive needs to make more honey. A cloud of worker bees buzzes around the hive. They are getting ready to look for more food. The little honeybee is with them. This is what she was born to do. She will spend the rest of her life flying in search of food for her big family.

Little Lizard

Written by Jennifer Boudart

Illustrated by Gary Torrisi

A baby lizard climbs out of her egg, buried beneath the sands of the tropical rain forest. She used a special tooth to break out of the hard shell of her egg. Now she must explore her surroundings.

Little Lizard is a green iguana lizard, but her sharp claws and the scales along her back make her look a lot like a tiny dragon.

In the rain forest, the sunlight filters through the leafy treetops and bounces off her green skin. She shines like a jewel.

Other lizards crawl around in the sand. They are Little Lizard's brothers and sisters. Soon the forest floor is covered with baby lizards. They all want to explore their new world.

A curious toucan sits on a branch high above the ground. It watches the lizards crawl across the sand, looking for food.

Baby lizards are not raised by a mother or father lizard. Young lizards are born knowing what they have to do to survive in the rain forest. Knowing how to survive without being told is called instinct.

Little Lizard is still small enough to fit in a human hand. She could grow up to be six feet long when she's older, though!

Little Lizard is dazzled by all of the interesting sounds of the rain forest. She hears the water falling, and she hears the birds calling to each other through the forest.

Little Lizard flicks her long tongue and bobs her head. Lizards have amazing tongues! They use their tongues to zap their food, clean their eyes, smell, and even scare away enemies. In front of Little Lizard, an army of ants carries leaves across the sandy floor of the forest.

Now Little Lizard is hungry. She leads a group of lizards across a trail of leaves. A quick movement catches her eye. Gulp! Little Lizard extends her long tongue and snaps up her first meal: a tasty termite. She eats a few more termites before moving on.

The lizards climb up a big tree near the river. The green leaves hide them well.

Some lizards are called chameleons. This means that their skin changes colors to match their surroundings. Then they stay hidden from enemies. Little Lizard is not a chameleon. Her skin is always green to match the green leaves of the rainforest.

A dark shadow passes over the lizards' hiding spot on the mangrove tree. It is a hawk on the hunt. The hawk flies over the branch that Little Lizard is resting on.

She naturally knows just what she has to do. Her claws let go of the tree branch. Little Lizard is falling! She hits the water with a splash.

Little Lizard's tail comes in handy. It helps her balance as she walks, swims, or runs. Some lizards use their tails to escape from enemies. The tail breaks off at a special point and keeps twitching as the lizard gets away. Don't worry! Soon the lizard will grow a new tail.

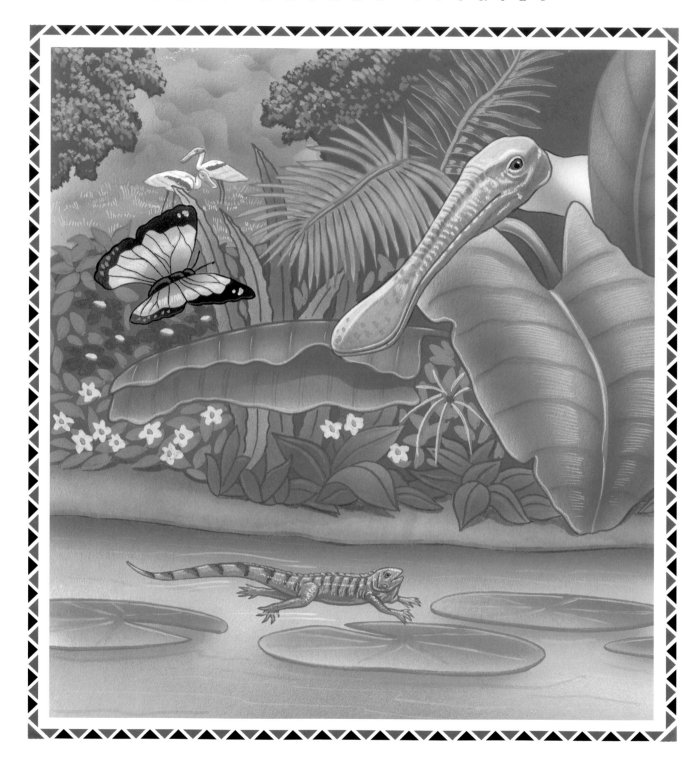

Little Lizard is a very good swimmer. She paddles toward a water lily and climbs on the leaf. Her long legs carry her from lily pad to lily pad. She reaches the shore and keeps on running.

Little Lizard hops over to a fallen tree trunk. All the other lizards are gone. Little Lizard seems to be alone now, but she is safe.

Little Lizard is surrounded by more strange animals. But she knows that these animals won't hurt her. She jumps onto a tree branch hanging over the water.

Suddenly, Little Lizard discovers she is not alone, and not at all safe. The tree trunk under her starts to roll! Little Lizard sees that the tree trunk is really a tapir, a forest animal that looks like a pig with a long snout. She leaps onto a nearby tree and escapes from danger.

The tapir moves on to a better resting place, too, as Little Lizard scampers quickly across the branch.

Little Lizard needs to find more food. She jumps from tree to tree looking for insects and a safe place to rest.

Little Lizard is safe at last! But wait. She is not the only lizard in this tree. Another lizard rests on a higher branch. But he is full-grown, four feet long, and he's not about to share his hideout.

The adult lizard swings his long tail. Clearly, the young lizard is not welcome in this tree! Little Lizard jumps out of the tree.

Little Lizard could grow to be as big as this lizard or even bigger. Some lizards grow to be six feet long!

Little Lizard is back on the ground again. This is not where she wants to be! Iguanas like to be high in the trees, where they can warm themselves in the sun.

Little Lizard looks up, searching for her special place. She looks right into the eyes of a jaguar! The jaguar growls loudly at her. Then Little Lizard is off and running again.

This jaguar probably wouldn't hurt Little Lizard. But she doesn't want to take any chances. Again, she searches for something to eat and a safe place to rest.

Little Lizard finally finds a safe place. This bush has plenty of delicious fruit for her to eat. It looks like Little Lizard will be just fine after all.

Tiny Gosling

Written by Jennifer Boudart

Illustrated by Anastasia Mitchell

Two geese guard a nest of eggs. One of the geese is bigger than the other. He is the gander, or male goose. The gander guards the smaller goose. She is his mate for life.

Mother Goose sits down on her nest while the gander stands guard. The gander is the father of the baby geese that are growing inside the eggs. They are almost ready to hatch.

Mother Goose has kept the eggs warm for almost one month, turning them each day. This helps the baby geese, or goslings, grow properly in their eggs. Today the eggs are starting to hatch!

The first egg cracks open. Tiny Gosling's little orange beak pokes through the egg. Next, his head pokes out of the shell. Tiny Gosling must break out of the hard shell without any help from Mother Goose or Father Gander.

Finally, Tiny Gosling pushes his body out of the egg. His feathers are very wet. Tiny Gosling blinks his eyes and lies on his side to rest. He is very tired. Tiny Gosling's brothers and sisters are breaking free of their eggs, too. One by one, little goslings push their way out of their shells. All ten eggs hatch in one day.

Tiny Gosling and the others are dry in a few hours. The nest is full of fuzzy, little goslings! Mother Goose has lined the nest with small, soft feathers from her body, called down. During their first hours of life, she covers her new family with her body to protect them.

When she leaves the nest, Mother Goose covers her goslings with straw and feathers to keep them warm and safe. Father Gander keeps other animals away from the nest by flapping his wings and honking. This is a signal for the other animals to stay away!

Now that Tiny Gosling and his brothers and sisters are warm and dry, they need to eat! Goslings can feed themselves from the time they are born. Mother Goose leads the goslings into the barnyard. She shows them how to pull at the grass and weeds.

Sometimes the farmer lets the geese snack on weeds for him! The edges of a goose's bill are shaped like a saw. That makes it easier to tear plants. While Tiny Gosling eats, he swallows bits of stone and dirt with his food. These bits don't hurt Tiny Gosling, but help grind the food into small pieces. Then the geese can digest their food easier.

In the morning, Mother Goose takes the goslings to the pond. Goslings can swim when they are only one day old. Tiny Gosling is the first one to go into the pond. He dips his head under first. Then he dips his whole body. Tiny Gosling shakes his feathers as the water trickles down his back.

Tiny Gosling moves into deeper water and begins paddling with his tiny, webbed feet. He is swimming! Soon all his brothers and sisters join him. As they swim, they take small sips of water with their beaks and lift their heads so the water can slide down their long necks.

Now Tiny Gosling is almost eight weeks old. He has new feathers and looks more like his parents, but he will not be full-grown until he is almost two years old! Although he will be able to fly soon, Tiny Gosling will never fly away. The farm is his home. Sometimes geese act as watchdogs for the farmer!

One day, Tiny Gosling sees a strange animal. It is a cat, looking for food. When the stranger approaches, Tiny Gosling springs into action. He runs at the cat with his neck stretched out and his wings flapping. He honks and hisses as loud as he can. The cat runs away!

When the big cat has gone away, Tiny Gosling settles down and begins to rub his beak over his feathers. He starts near the base of his tail and collects a special oil onto his beak, then spreads the oil over his feathers. This is called preening.

Tiny Gosling does this again and again. He takes his time so he will not miss any spots. This oil keeps his feathers waterproof. Tiny Gosling takes good care of his feathers to keep them clean and neat. He pulls out dead feathers and picks off tiny bugs. Tiny Gosling cleans his feathers so they will keep him warm in the winter.

When Tiny Gosling's feathers are clean and dry he walks over to the farmer's lawn for a snack. He waddles through the barnyard, watching the other geese settle down for an afternoon nap. Tiny Gosling is not tired just yet.

In the farmer's front yard, Tiny Gosling sees a friendly butterfly. Then he sees the crunchy weeds popping up from the farmer's yard! He waddles toward the tasty weeds.

Just then, the farmer's dog comes around the corner of the house. Tiny Gosling doesn't see this big dog coming toward him at all!

The farmer's dog is watching Tiny Gosling. The dog knows that the goose should not be grazing without the farmer's permission.

Suddenly the dog runs after Tiny Gosling. The little goose runs toward the barnyard, flapping his tiny wings. Tiny Gosling is scared, but this dog won't hurt him.

As Tiny Gosling reaches the barnyard, the farmer's dog runs back to the house. Tiny Gosling is definitely tired now. Maybe he should take a nap after all.

When Tiny Gosling is not bathing or eating, he is sleeping. He tucks his head behind his wing. His round eye opens lazily from time to time. Life on the farm is good for this young goose.

Tiny Tiger

Written by Jennifer Boudart

Illustrated by Krista Brauckmann-Towns

It is morning in the jungle. Steam rises up from the ground. Jungle plants sparkle with dew. Monkeys and birds chatter in the treetops. It's a morning just like any other morning. Or is it?

Look! Three tiger cubs come tumbling out of their dark cave. Today is their first day outdoors. They are eight weeks old and ready to explore.

The cubs' whiskers twitch as they move through the tall grasses and leaves. A tiger's whiskers are almost as sensitive as fingertips. They help a tiger avoid objects, judge spaces, and feel its way in the dark.

The bright sun makes the cubs blink. Their eyes are used to the darkness of the cave. A monkey screams, and two cubs scramble for cover.

The third cub is a little smaller, but much braver, than her brothers. She looks for the noisy monkey swinging through the trees.

Her name is Tiny Tiger, and one day she will grow up to be a beautiful tigress.

Tigers' eyes work well even in low light, so tigers are nocturnal, meaning they are most active at night.

A low grunting sound brings all three cubs running. The cubs know the familiar sound of their mother's voice.

Tiny Tiger and her brothers follow Mother Tiger through the tall jungle grass. Their stripes hide them very well. To other animals, they look like swaying grasses filled with shadows and sunlight.

Every tiger's stripes are unique. A tiger's face markings are so distinctive that they can be used to tell two tigers apart.

Tiny Tiger is amazed by the world around her. There is so much to see, smell, and hear!

Tiny Tiger sees her mother's long, swinging tail. She tries to catch it! Mother holds her tail high out of her baby's reach. Tiny Tiger doesn't use her claws. That would hurt Mother Tiger! Tigers' claws are retractable, which means they can be withdrawn into a tiger's paw like a turtle's head is pulled into its shell.

Tiny Tiger turns to chase her own tail. Round in circles she goes. Her mother grunts softly. Keep moving!

The tiger family comes upon a small lake. It is quiet, cool, and shady—perfect for the hot tigers. First, Mother Tiger checks the area for danger. No jackals or jaguars. Just a few harmless little birds. Mother Tiger heads for the water, and her cubs follow her.

The three young tiger cubs have never been swimming. Like all tigers, the three cubs love water. They march right in!

Tigers don't like hot weather. They will often cool themselves off by lying in shallow pools of cool water.

The little cubs wrestle and tumble by the cool jungle lake. Tiger cubs play games that are good practice for hunting. They also learn to stalk, chase, and pounce by watching their mother.

Tiny Tiger sees a colorful peacock. She takes a few steps toward the beautiful bird. It flies away! Tiny Tiger thinks the peacock is afraid of her. But she is wrong.

The bird has seen something large in the grass. Suddenly a loud roar freezes Tiny Tiger in her tracks!

There is another tiger here! The cubs run and hide behind their mother. Mother Tiger is not scared because she knows this visitor. He is Father Tiger. They rub necks to say hello.

Tiny Tiger bravely jumps from behind her mother. She growls a baby growl. Her father gently rubs her with his big paw before going on his way.

Tiny Tiger won't always have Mother Tiger to protect her. A tiger cub will leave its mother after two years to find its own territory. There, the cub will spend most of its life hunting and living alone.

Tiny Tiger is a playful cub. She creeps slowly and quietly to practice hunting. Her little body stays low to the ground, and her ears press flat against her head. Suddenly she jumps! She has caught a peacock feather!

One day, Tiny Tiger will catch real food. Tigers are carnivores, meaning they hunt for their food and eat meat. Today is just for fun, though. Her brothers chase her, trying to steal her prize.

Tiny Tiger runs to Mother Tiger and shows her the colorful peacock feather.

The family returns home for a short nap. The cubs cuddle together in front of their cave. Mother Tiger washes each of the three cubs with her rough tongue. Then she lies down with them to rest.

If the cubs try to wander off, Mother Tiger will bring them back. Mother Tiger can carry her cubs by gently grabbing a cub's neck in her mouth. Loose folds of skin on the top of a cub's neck are a natural handle for Mother Tiger.

After her nap, Mother Tiger hunts for food for her little cubs. She leaves them safely napping near the cave.

Tiny Tiger's legs kick as she sleeps. She flicks her tail and growls softly. She dreams of the day when she will grow up to roam the jungle as a mighty tigress.

Baby Pig

Written by Lenaya Raack

Illustrated by Kathy Rusynyk

A pair of big brown eyes peek through the wooden fence in the barn. A young girl kneels in the hay and watches Mother Pig feed her new litter of piglets. The girl stays quiet. She counts the tiny tails—one, two, three…all the way up to nine.

The girl gets up and quietly moves around to the other side. Now the girl can see all of the piglets. They are all perfectly pink—except for the littlest one on the end. She has brown spots all over her body. This is the little girl's favorite piglet. She calls her Baby Pig.

Baby Pig moves with her family to a new home. It is called a sty or pigpen. It has a fence around it and hay on the ground. Baby Pig lives here with Mother and Father Pig and her sisters and brothers. At night, the piglets sleep close together to stay warm. Sometimes they even sleep on top of one another.

Today, Baby Pig wakes up first. She sniffs the ground looking for food. She is hungry all the time. Suddenly Baby Pig hears the girl coming. Baby Pig watches her pour the food into a long wooden bucket called a trough. Now all of the pigs are awake. Baby Pig has to push past the other hungry pigs to eat.

Today, Baby Pig and her family are going into the barnyard with the other animals. Baby Pig likes the barnyard, because it is much bigger than the sty. There is more room for her to run and play.

The girl opens the gate of the pigpen. One by one, the piglets follow their mother and father into the barnyard. A curious calf comes up to sniff Baby Pig. She doesn't mind. She wants to play, but Mother Pig grunts loudly and the calf moves away.

Baby Pig walks over to the fence, sniffing the ground for food. The girl comes over and says, "Are you hungry, Baby Pig? Here's a treat for you." The little girl gives the pig an apple.

It is summertime on the farm and very hot. The ground is dry and dusty. In the shade of the barn, the chickens roll in the dust to keep their feathers from sticking together. Baby Pig doesn't sweat, so she needs to roll in the mud to get cool.

Soon the girl brings out a hose and makes a big mud hole by squirting water on the dirt. Baby Pig is the first one to jump in. She rolls and wriggles and splashes until she is covered in mud. She's not hot anymore. The other pigs follow Baby Pig. They run and jump into the mud, too. Soon all the pigs are the color of mud. The little girl laughs. "I can hardly see you in all that mud," she says.

Baby Pig is looking for something good to eat. She walks over to where the chickens are eating, but she doesn't want to eat grain. She walks over to where the cows are eating, but she doesn't want to eat hay.

Maybe there is something good to eat in the barn. Baby Pig sticks her head in a pail, but it is empty. She tries to pull her head out, but the pail won't come off! Baby Pig shakes her head, but the pail doesn't move. She begins to run. The chickens and roosters see Baby Pig and run away. The geese see her, too, and honk and fly up on the fence. Splash! Baby Pig lands in the mud. Finally the pail pops off!

Sometimes, the girl takes Baby Pig for walks. Today, they're going for a short walk down the road. Baby Pig likes to go for walks, because there are lots of new things for her to see. She watches a squirrel run up a tree and a rabbit hop into a bush.

Baby Pig stops to smell the yellow flowers that grow along the road. As they walk farther up the road, they see dogs herding a large flock of sheep. Baby Pig wants to help, but the girl tells her, "No, Baby Pig, pigs don't herd sheep."

Then they stop under an apple tree to rest. The girl feeds Baby Pig an apple for being so good.

Baby Pig is hungry again. This time, Baby Pig tries the corn growing in the field. She squeezes under the fence and races for the big cornstalks. Baby Pig knocks over a cornstalk and eats the ears of corn.

Soon Baby Pig sees a rabbit hopping around the cornstalks and chases it. Baby Pig wants to play, but the rabbit disappears down a hole. Now Baby Pig is lost. The corn is too tall! Baby Pig can't see the barnyard.

Then Baby Pig hears a familiar voice. It's the girl! Baby Pig squeals and the girl comes running to find her.

Baby Pig is five months old now. She's too big to be picked up and carried by the girl. But she likes to follow the girl around the barnyard while the girl does her chores. She watches as the girl throws grain on the ground and the chickens gobble it up.

Then Baby Pig follows the girl into the barn. The girl climbs up a ladder into the hayloft. She throws hay down to the barn floor to feed the cows. The girl doesn't notice the hay falling on top of Baby Pig. Baby Pig is covered in hay. When the girl sees the pig in the hay, she giggles playfully and says, "Sorry, Baby Pig."

The farm is quiet. It is nighttime, now. In the barn, the cows sleepily eat one last mouthful of hay. The calves are already asleep in their stalls. The hens are sitting on their nests in the hen house. Their chicks are safely tucked under their mothers' feathers. Outside, the pigs are back in their sty. They are lying down and getting ready to sleep, too.

The barnyard is dark and empty now. The farmhouse is quiet. Baby Pig and the girl sit on the bottom step of the porch. They watch the fireflies blinking on and off in the darkness. When it is time for bed, the girl walks Baby Pig back to her pen and gives her a good-night hug.

Now Baby Pig is one year old. Soon she will have her own babies. Every day the girl brings food and stops to talk to her.

When the new piglets are born, the girl chooses one to be her new pet. She knows this piglet is just as special as Baby Pig.

Bear Cub

Written by Sarah Toast

Illustrated by Krista Brauckmann-Towns

As summer draws to an end, Mother Bear roams through the mountain forest, gathering and eating enormous amounts of berries and fruit.

Mother Bear is putting on fat so she can sleep in her den the entire winter. The layer of fat will keep her warm and help her provide rich milk for the baby bear that will be born.

The air is turning cold. Mother Bear must hurry. She still has a lot of work to do. She must find a home for herself and her baby.

Mother Bear chooses a rocky cave to be her den during the winter. Inside the den, she and her baby will be protected from the cold wind and blowing snow. She pads it with moss, leaves, and grass to make it warm and soft for herself and the new baby.

As the first flakes of winter snow begin to fall, Mother Bear settles down and drifts off to sleep.

Soon the falling snow will build up outside and close off the den, keeping Mother Bear and her baby safe from harm.

In the middle of winter, when the snow drifts are deep outside the den, Mother Bear's tiny cub is born. With closed eyes and hardly any fur, the cub will grow quickly, nourished by Mother Bear's rich milk.

Baby Bear and Mother Bear sleep on, but Mother Bear will wake up and protect him if the winter home is disturbed.

Mother Bear sits or lies on her side in her den and keeps her cub warm by cuddling him close to her warm body.

In a few weeks, Baby Bear's eyes open. He is now covered in thick, soft fur. Mother Bear and Baby Bear stay in their snug den another month.

Bear cubs will stay in the den for three months before they venture outside. During these three months, they spend most of their time sleeping. They wake only to drink their mother's milk.

In the spring, Baby Bear and his mother emerge from the den. Mother Bear shows Baby Bear how to look through the forest for tender shoots that will make a good meal.

Mother Bear makes her way with Baby Bear down the grassy slope to the elks' winter range. She lifts up her head and sniffs the breeze. Baby Bear moves his raised head back and forth so hard that he falls right over.

Bears have such small eyes that people often assume they also have poor eyesight, but bears probably see as well as most humans.

Mother Bear finds an elk that died in the winter when the snows were deep and not enough food could be found.

Mother Bear eats as much as she can of the nourishing elk meat. Then she carefully buries it in a shallow hole and covers it with leaves, twigs, and dirt. She will return to it later.

Baby Bear learns by watching what his mother does. The most important rules for Baby Bear to learn are to follow mother, obey mother, and have fun.

Bear cubs stay with their mother about two years. During this time, they learn many survival tips, such as what to eat and how to escape danger, before they venture out on their own.

Mother Bear teaches her baby cub to turn over fallen branches and look for grubs to eat. With their long, sharp claws, Baby Bear and Mother Bear dig up bulbs, roots, and snails.

Bears will eat almost anything they can get their paws on, including grasses, berries, tree bark, plants, insects, some small mammals, and, of course, sweet honey!

When his mother stops to rest, Baby Bear likes to play. He climbs all over her. He somersaults into her lap and nibbles her ears, then runs off to chase a tiny field mouse.

When Mother Bear looks up from playing with her cub, she sees that a lean wolf is watching her and Baby Bear. Quickly she chases the cub into a hollow tree stump. Then she turns to face the wolf.

Mother Bear stands up on her hind legs, swings her front paws, and roars a loud growl. The wolf runs away.

Bears have five claws on each foot. They use their front paws for catching and holding prey, digging for insects and roots, and climbing trees.

Mother Bear calls to her cub, but he doesn't come out of the hollow stump. Mother Bear goes to find out why.

Baby Bear has found a treat. It is a honeycomb with honey from last summer still inside. Baby Bear sticks his little paw in the honeycomb and then licks it. He tastes the wildflowers of summer in the sweet honey.

As Baby Bear's first summer draws to an end, he is able to find his own food, although he might drink milk from Mother Bear occasionally. Now he must eat as much food as he can to prepare for his winter sleep.

When Baby Bear backs out of the hollow log, he brings some tasty honeycomb for his mother. She happily eats the honey, and then she and her cub give each other a true bear hug.

Little Jackrabbit

Written by Jim Strickler

Illustrated by Karen Pritchett

On a warm morning in the spring, Mother Jackrabbit is working quietly under the thick sagebrush. She is using her paw to scrape out a smooth spot in the dry, sandy soil.

Mother Jackrabbit covers the spot with some of her own fur to make a soft bed. Tucked under the sagebrush, the little bed is hidden from all other animals.

This bed is called a form. And soon Mother Jackrabbit will give birth to her babies here. This is why the bed must be so soft.

When the soft bed is ready, Mother Jackrabbit gives birth to three tiny baby jackrabbits. There are two girls and one boy. The boy jackrabbit is named Baby Jack.

Like his mother, Baby Jack has bright eyes, smooth brown fur, and a nose that constantly twitches. His big ears bounce up and down as he hops around the desert.

Jackrabbits' ears can be longer than their bodies. Also, their long ears keep them cool in the hot, desert sun. These long ears allow their heat to escape, cooling the body.

Even though he is young, Baby Jack is eager to explore his new world. His large ears pick up many wonderful sounds: the songs of a meadowlark, the barking of a prairie dog, and the "hooooo" of the wind blowing across the dry land.

As he sniffs the air, he enjoys smelling the sagebrush and the sweet cactus flowers.

Baby jackrabbits are born with fur on their tiny bodies. And they can hop about and explore their new world almost immediately after they are born!

During the hot desert days, Baby Jack does not explore. It is too hot for exploring when the sun is shining. Like his mother, he sits still in the cool shade of a clump of grass.

He feels safe in the shade. His brown fur blends right in with the soil and the dry grass. Hungry coyotes and eagles that are hunting for food cannot see him easily.

If an animal did come after Baby Jack, he would wait for the right moment. Then, in a flash, he would run away and find another safe hiding place in the grass.

In the desert, almost every day is bright, dry, and sunny. But this afternoon, Baby Jack watches gray clouds gather in the sky. The day gets cooler and darker. Then, Baby Jack feels drops of water coming from above. It is raining!

Rainy days are rare in the dry desert. The rain is new to Baby Jack. He hides behind a rock when the thunder sounds and the lightning flashes across the sky.

The rain puddles are quickly soaked up by the dry ground. The rain doesn't last very long. Soon the sun will come out again.

The rainfall changes the way the desert looks. It makes all the plants blossom. Instead of being brown and dry, the desert is now filled with many different kinds of colorful flowers.

Baby Jack explores the desert and sees things that he has never seen before. He is amazed to see so many beautiful colors: green, yellow, orange, pink, and purple.

Baby Jack looks at the beautiful flowers and sees good things to eat everywhere! He hops to find his family. Soon they will feast on all of the plants and flowers.

As the bright sun begins to set each evening, Baby Jack and his family search for food. He hops from plant to plant, nibbling on grasses. With his sharp teeth, he can eat almost anything.

Mother Jackrabbit teaches Baby Jack to chew a hole in a cactus. He avoids the prickly spines on the outside and eats the moist part inside.

Jackrabbits eat all kinds of plant material, including the inner bark of trees. Also, they feed mostly at night when it is cooler. And their enemies can't see the jackrabbits that well when it's dark outside.

After Baby Jack enjoys his tasty cactus meal, he and his mother do some more exploring. Mother Jackrabbit's powerful sense of smell helps her sniff out danger. She can smell a coyote approaching.

Baby Jack is playing around in the dirt when his mother sees the coyote watching them from a nearby rock.

Mother Jackrabbit knows what she must do. Jackrabbits use their hind feet to pound the ground and signal danger to each other. When jackrabbits hear this sound, they know that danger is quickly approaching. They must make a fast escape.

Baby Jack hears a loud "Thumpa, thumpa, thumpa!" Mother Jackrabbit is pounding one of her back paws against the hard ground.

Mother Jackrabbit is trying to tell Baby Jack and the other jackrabbits that danger is near. Baby Jack knows what it means. He must hide. Baby Jack immediately darts under a bushy plant.

Baby Jack will wait here until the danger is gone. The coyote sniffs around the bushes trying to pick up the jackrabbit scent.

The coyote leaves when he can't find any of the hiding jackrabbits. Baby Jack tenses his powerful leg muscles. Then—whoosh—he is off! He bounds away to meet up with his family.

Goat Kids

Written by Catherine McCafferty

Illustrated by Andrea Tachiera

Goat twins Billy and Nanny stand up in the hay as the farmer comes into the barn. The farmer always comes early in the morning to milk the mama goat.

Today, when the farmer is finished, he pats Nanny and Billy. "You two will have to look after yourselves today," the farmer says. He leads their mother away. Mama Goat will care for a newborn lamb whose own mother can't take care of it.

What will Billy and Nanny do today? Billy likes to eat. Nanny likes to jump and climb. But they also like to stay together.

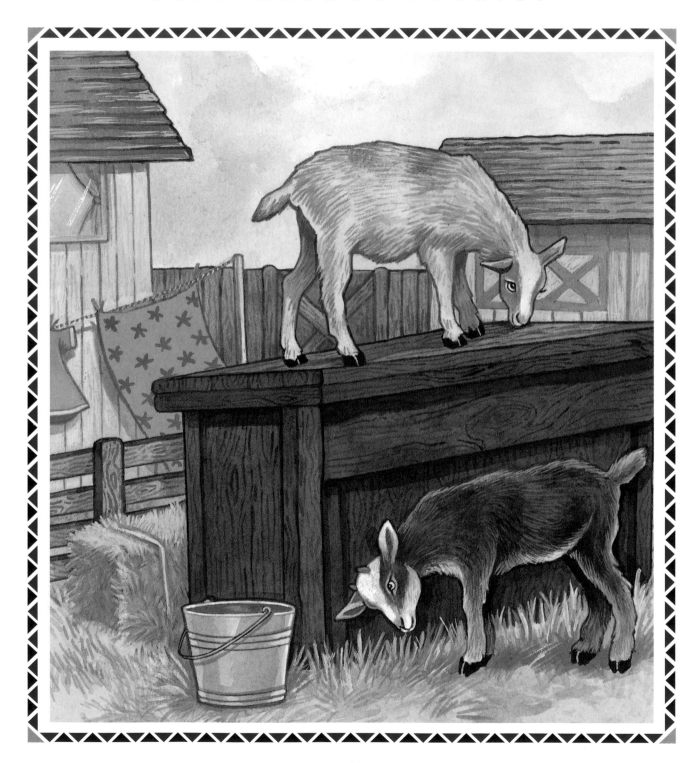

Billy and Nanny nibble happily from the hay bin. They have had their teeth since they were born. And that's a good thing since Billy likes to eat all the time.

Nanny ventures out into the barnyard. Suddenly she sees that the shed roof is just the right height for climbing. Nanny hops onto a hay bale, then leans her front hooves against the shed and jumps up.

Soon Billy joins her. Their two-toed feet and sturdy hooves keep them sure-footed. Like all goats, they have strong legs and good balance.

Nanny and Billy look around the farm from the top of the shed roof. They like being up where they can see everything.

High places are good lookouts for goats. If goats think danger is coming, they spread out and climb to high places to spot it. Then they leap down to surprise any approaching enemies.

Billy and Nanny don't see any danger. But they do see that the roof slopes right down into the farmer's yard. Billy thinks that he might get a snack there.

After climbing carefully down the other side of the roof, Billy and Nanny land in the farmer's yard. Their "shock absorbers" in the inside layers of their feet keep them from hurting their legs when they land.

Billy stops at the farmer's kitchen door. He climbs the three little steps to the back porch and waits for the door to open. Nanny climbs up the steps, then down again. She does this a few times, then goes to find a higher place to climb. When Nanny gets to the farmer's pick-up truck, she jumps onto the hood and then onto the roof. She climbs just the way mountain goats do, as if she is jumping from one narrow ledge to another.

Suddenly Billy sees the farmer. "Okay, you two," the farmer says, "I have a better place for you." The farmer leads Billy and Nanny to a big field. The field is covered with bushes and thick brush. Other goats are already munching on the heavy undergrowth. Billy sees delicious food everywhere he looks.

Billy's first feeding stop is a thick, prickly bush. Billy expects the plant to be tender, but his tough mouth feels prickles instead. If Billy's mother was with him, she would eat the toughest parts of the plant, and leave the tender parts for Billy and Nanny. Billy does the best he can to get at the tender parts.

Billy is so busy eating that he does not notice Nanny wandering off. With the other goats around, Nanny doesn't mind being a little farther away from Billy. Nanny tries to run and leap in the field, but it is too crowded with other goats.

At the far end of the field, Nanny sees a fence. She trots toward it. The fence does not look too high. Nanny leaps and sails over the fence into a grassy field. Then she jumps back into the brushy field. Then back over the fence again. When Nanny has jumped enough, she settles down to munch for a while in the grassy field.

Nanny doesn't see the cows munching nearby. But then she hears a loud "Mooooooo!" Nanny crouches low to the ground as heavy footsteps get closer. She hears the cow's loud chewing. Nanny peeks up and sees a cow for the first time!

Nanny runs and runs across the grassy field to get away from the big animal, but then sees other animals like it all through the field. Nanny hops over a fence at the other side of the field. When she stops running, Nanny is far away from the cows. But she is also far away from Billy and the other goats. Nanny tries to find a lookout spot, but the field is flat and open.

Suddenly, Nanny sees her mother and leaps to her side. Mama Goat stands over a newborn lamb. Woolly, round animals peer at Nanny, but she is safe now. At the end of the day, the farmer is very surprised to see Nanny with her mother. The farmer pats Nanny on the head, and leads Nanny and her mother back toward the brushy field.

In the field, Billy is as full as he can be. The goats have done a good job of clearing all the tough brush from the field. The farmer leads all the goats back toward the barn.

Back in the barn, Nanny settles down in the hay. She is tired from her busy day of jumping and exploring the farm.

Billy is so full that he doesn't even go to the hay or grain bins. He sits near Nanny in the soft hay. Their mother joins them. It has been a busy day for all of them. Mama Goat has helped the baby lamb. Billy has helped the farmer clear the field. And Nanny has met cows and sheep for the very first time!

The three of them curl up in the hay and sleep soundly all night long.

The next morning, Nanny and Billy find some large wooden blocks stacked next to a tree. They carefully climb up the blocks. From there, Nanny can see everything and Billy can munch on the tree's tender leaves. Now they can do what they like best—together!

Baby Kangaroo

Written by Jennifer Boudart

Illustrated by Linda Holt Ayriss

The red gum tree shades the Australian outback on warm afternoons.

Kangaroos know this well, so they rest under the trees during the hot summer days. They lie on their sides, with their long legs stretched out behind them.

One kangaroo does not want to take a nap. His name is Joey, and he wants to play.

A kangaroo is a marsupial, which means the mother kangaroo carries her baby in a warm pouch on her belly.

A kangaroo is called a joey when it is a baby. Joey is only a few months old. Like all kangaroos, he has strong back legs, large feet, and a long tail. When Joey moves, it's easy to see why his legs and body are so big and strong.

He hops! Joey bounces along on his back legs, using his tail for balance.

A kangaroo can jump seven feet into the air with one bounce!

Some kangaroos can grow as tall as six feet. And from nose to tail tip, some kangaroos measure ten feet long!

Joey finds two other young kangaroos who are awake, too. They start to wrestle each other, poking tummies and tugging on ears and tails. Little Joey leads the others in a hopping race.

A clucking noise makes him stop suddenly. It is his mother calling him. She uses the sound to tell Joey that he has wandered too far from her. Joey quickly returns to his mother.

A group of kangaroos traveling together is called a mob. It consists of one adult male, two or three females, and their young.

Joey is very tired after all of his fun and games. He climbs headfirst into a small pouch located in his mother's tummy. The pouch is the perfect size for her baby. Only Joey's legs are sticking out. Then he turns himself around in the pouch so he can see.

A kangaroo mother's pouch makes a great built-in bed for her babies.

Joey knows this pouch very well, because he spends a lot of time here. A joey usually lives in its mother's pouch until it's too big to fit inside—about one year.

An adult kangaroo stamps its foot on the ground. That sound means danger! Joey's mother lifts her head and sniffs the air. Suddenly, a dingo dog comes running from the trees.

The kangaroos must escape! Quickly, they jump away, flying through the air. Joey ducks down into his mother's pouch. His mother has never moved so fast!

Adult kangaroos traveling quickly can cover distances up to 27 feet with each bounce, and they can reach speeds of 40 miles per hour.

Mother Kangaroo jumps fast and far. The pack of dingo dogs can't keep up. Soon the dingoes drop back. The kangaroos are safe, but they keep on moving. They are heading toward a patch of rain clouds.

The kangaroos know that tasty green grass grows wherever rain has fallen. The group reaches its new home before dark.

A kangaroo's most important senses are smell and hearing. They have long ear flaps which they can turn backward and forward to hear sounds from all directions.

The kangaroos settle into their new home. Night is coming, and it is getting cooler. Joey and the other kangaroos will spend the evening feeding.

Joey's mother nibbles some grass. She uses her short front arms and big back feet to hop-step forward. Joey is still in her pouch. He learns to eat by watching his mother. When she stretches down to eat some grass or nibble on leaves, he stretches down to eat some grass, too.

At six months, a joey begins to eat grass and leaves, but it still drinks its mother's milk.

Joey's little tummy is now full. Joey leaves his mother's pouch. It is grooming time. He uses a paw to comb the fur on his legs, arms, tummy, chest, back, and floppy ears. He licks his arms and rubs them over his face.

Grooming keeps Joey clean, and it also keeps the biting bugs away. When Joey is all finished grooming, he looks for a playmate.

Kangaroos can keep cool by licking their forearms. When this skin is moistened, the blood underneath is cooled. This blood then travels to the rest of the body and cools it, too.

Joey hops to a pool filled with fresh rainwater. The pool is new to him. The land where he lives is normally very dry. Joey looks into the water. He sees another kangaroo looking back at him! Who is this strange kangaroo?

Joey leans closer to look in the water at the stranger's face. Oops! Joey dips his nose in the water and gets all wet.

Kangaroos can cool themselves by taking a dip in the water, too. Joey looks around and sees some older kangaroos splashing around in the cool water.

The water feels wonderful. Joey hops right into the puddle. Soon other young kangaroos join him there. They discover what the older kangaroos already know—water is fun!

Farm Kitten

Written by Catherine McCafferty

Illustrated by Debbie Pinkney

Today is a special day! In a warm, quiet corner of the barn Mama Cat nestles in the hay and gives birth to five kittens. Mama Cat dries Farm Kitten and his sisters' wet fur with her tongue.

Even though their eyes aren't open, the kittens use their sense of smell to find their favorite spot to nurse each time they eat. Nursing is important since Mama Cat's milk keeps the kittens from getting sick.

As the kittens get older, Mama Cat will teach them how to become mousers and help the farmer. Mousers catch mice and rats that eat the farmer's corn and grains.

Farm Kitten is two weeks old now. His eyes are open and he can hear. But Farm Kitten still stays close to Mama Cat. He mews to his sisters, and they sleep together in a pile of warmth and comfort when their mother is out hunting for food.

Mama Cat leaves her kittens safe in the barn when she goes out to catch a mouse or a rat.

Mama Cat has caught a rat today. Back at the barn, she shows her kittens how she caught it. All of the kittens will need to hunt for themselves someday. Farm Kitten watches his mother very carefully.

Farm Kitten is four weeks old and ready to explore. He steps out from his soft bed of hay. There are so many new sounds and sights and smells!

Farm Kitten hears a noise in one of the stalls. He jumps up on the stall divider and swings his tail sideways to keep his balance. In the stall, he sees a huge brown cow! What a big animal! He fluffs up the hair on his back and tail, and hisses as loud as he can. The big cow just keeps chewing her hay. She is not scared of Farm Kitten.

Farm Kitten looks down from his high place. He stretches as far as he can toward the ground, then slides the rest of the way down the stall.

Out in the barnyard, Farm Kitten smells the muddy wallow that the pigs are enjoying. As Farm Kitten tries to get a closer look, one of the pigs trots by him. Splish! Splat! Farm Kitten is all muddy!

Farm Kitten finds a quiet spot to wash himself. He wants to remove the mud and the scent of the pigs from his fur. Smells are very important to cats, and Farm Kitten doesn't want to be mistaken for a pig! Plus, washing helps to calm Farm Kitten.

He licks his paw and then wipes his face with it. Farm Kitten tugs at the fur between the pads of his feet to get all of the mud out. A clean, fluffy coat will keep Farm Kitten warm and dry.

When Farm Kitten is finished grooming, he sees his mother down by the pond with the rest of the kittens. At last, Farm Kitten can watch her hunt. But this is a different kind of hunting. Farm Kitten pricks up his ears and watches his mother closely.

His mother looks down in the water for a long time. Suddenly, she darts her paw under the water and throws a flipping, flopping fish up on the grass!

Farm Kitten has never seen a fish before. It splashes him when it moves. Farm Kitten doesn't like getting wet any more than he likes getting muddy. But he tries to hunt, anyway. He dips his paw in the water, scaring all of the fish away.

Mama Cat doesn't want Farm Kitten to be so close to the water. She picks him up by the scruff of his neck and carries him away from the pond. Kittens have loose skin around their necks so Mama Cat can carry them without hurting them.

Farm Kitten's sisters rush over to him once their mother sets him down. It's playtime! Farm Kitten finds a dragonfly. The other kittens wrestle with one another, trying to hold on with their front paws while they kick with their back paws.

Kicking with their back paws protects their soft stomachs. Their mother has taught them this from the time they were very young.

Stalking in the grass, they practice creeping up on one another. They crouch down low and wait for just the right moment to pounce. Farm Kitten pounces again and again. Sometimes he catches his sister. But sometimes he misses!

Suddenly, Farm Kitten spots a crow pecking in the grass. Farm Kitten stays low in the grass. He waves his tail in the air. Farm Kitten's swishing tail gives him away. The crow's sharp eyes see the tail as a warning, and the bird flies away. Farm Kitten tries to pounce, but all he catches is a pawful of air.

Maybe next time, Farm Kitten!

Farm Kitten's wagging tail has attracted one of the farm puppies. Even though Farm Kitten and the puppy are both baby animals, they have different body signals.

The puppy doesn't know that Farm Kitten wags his tail when he is angry. Puppies wag their tails when they are happy.

When Farm Kitten raises his paw to swat the puppy away, the puppy wants to play. The puppy barks, wanting to join in a game. Farm Kitten climbs up a tree to get away from the puppy. There, he waits for the puppy to go away.

It has been a busy day, and Farm Kitten is ready for a nap. His senses of sight and smell work together to help him find his way back to the barn.

Suddenly, Farm Kitten hears a high-pitched squeak. He pricks up his ears and walks slowly into the barn. It is dark inside, but Farm Kitten can see just fine. Cats have special eyes that help them see in dim light.

Just then, Farm Kitten spots a rat at the end of the barn! He creeps closer, using his whiskers to tell him when he is getting too close to objects in the barn. Farm Kitten doesn't want to bump into things and scare away the rat before he can pounce.

Farm Kitten leaps at the rat—but misses! It runs off into the hay. Maybe Farm Kitten will catch a rat tomorrow. Now he is sleepy.

Farm Kitten crawls back to his soft bed and gently falls to sleep. He dreams of becoming a true mouser one day.

Snowy Owl

Written by Sarah Toast

Illustrated by Kevin Torline

The long winter's snow is just beginning to melt away as Mother Snowy Owl scrapes a shallow nest on top of a very small hill. In spring it is cold on the Arctic tundra.

The ground is still wet, so Mother Owl lines the nest with moss and feathers. She settles into the nest, then she calls to Father Snowy Owl.

Father Snowy Owl must take good care of Mother Owl for the next few months. She has a very big job to do, and Father Owl is going to help.

Mother Owl lays a glossy white egg in the nest and sits on top of it, sharing the warmth of her body with the egg. Father Owl brings a lemming for Mother Owl to eat. He brings food to her so she doesn't have to leave the nest.

The next day, Mother Owl lays another white egg, and two days after that another, until there are eight eggs in the nest.

Mother Owl's feathers are mostly white. Her white feathers help Mother Owl blend in with the snow that makes up her environment.

The springtime wildflowers bloom bright as Mother Owl sits patiently on the nest. She and Father Owl call to each other to keep in touch.

As the long spring days pass, Father Owl makes many flights to hunt for lemmings and hares. He flies swiftly and silently. Father Owl brings back meals caught in his sharp claws.

The lemmings that Father Owl caught are mouse-size animals that burrow beneath the snow in the late fall, winter, and early spring. They come out in the warmer months.

Other tundra animals—arctic foxes and weasels, falcons and hawks—are also hunting for the lemmings. Father Owl competes with foxes and wolves when he hunts for hares.

Father Owl has excellent hearing and eyesight which helps him to spy prey first. His eyes are very large. And although he can't move his eyes around very much, his head is very flexible.

Father Owl can sneak up on his prey, too. His feathers are extremely light, so when he flies he makes no sound. His prey can't run away because they don't hear him coming.

Finally the first tiny owlet hatches out of the first egg laid by Mother Owl. This first little owl is called Baby Snowy, and he is covered with soft white down.

As soon as Snowy is able to eat, Father and Mother Owl feed him tender bits they have stored nearby. The next day, another owlet hatches. After ten days, Snowy has seven brothers and sisters.

Owls eat insects, birds, and small mammals. But owls cannot digest bones and fur, so after they're done eating they bring up small pellets of bone and fur.

A caribou wanders too close to the family's nest. Mother and Father Owl shrill "krick-krick, krick-krick" to drive him off. Snowy also tries his hardest to "krick-krick."

The caribou looks up from his grazing. When the caribou turns away from the nest, Father Owl calls out a loud "ho-ho."

Father Owl's call could probably be heard from very far away. His loud call let the caribou know that he has come too close to the nest. The caribou eats some more grass and then walks away.

Caribou are visitors to the tundra during the summertime, but shaggy musk oxen live there all year round. Musk oxen and caribou eat the grasses, leaves, and mosses that abound in the long days of summer.

Snowy and his family watch the musk oxen. Like other owls, Snowy can turn his head around to see what's behind him.

Most owls can turn their heads to face the backs of their bodies. And some owls can turn them even farther!

Snowy and his brothers and sisters are growing bigger daily. Mother Owl no longer needs to cover them in the nest. Mother Owl stands guard near the nest while Father Owl searches for a hare to feed the large family.

During the midsummer, when the Arctic nights are as light as day, Snowy steps out of the nest and spreads his wings.

Most owls are nocturnal, meaning they are active only at night when it's dark. But Snowy lives in the tundra where sometimes the sun shines all night.

Snowy steps slowly down the small hill. He is the first owlet in the family to climb over the rocks and walk through all of the wildflowers near the nest. He sees a snow goose gliding above him.

Snowy is so happy he hoots. Mother Owl and the owlets look over from the nest to make sure Snowy is safe.

One day, Snowy will be big enough to fly away from the nest and start his own family. He will always be smaller than his sisters, though. Male owls are smaller than female owls.

Snowy spends many hours exploring the frozen tundra around the nest. Day by day, his brothers and sisters become explorers, too, as they grow old enough to leave the nest.

Little Calf

Written by Lenaya Raack

Illustrated by Debbie Pinkney

The snow falls gently outside the barn. Inside, the animals are safe and dry. It is nighttime on the farm. In the dim light, hens cluck and settle down on their nests high up in the rafters. The horses close their eyes and give a final whinny.

In a far corner, a lantern glows like a firefly in the growing darkness. A young boy watches Mother Cow who is lying quietly on her side in the hay. It is time for her baby to be born.

Soon a sleepy calf lies beside Mother Cow. The boy names the calf Daisy. The calf sits quietly as Mother Cow cleans Daisy's wet fur.

Daisy is only fifteen minutes old. The boy watches as Mother Cow gives Daisy a gentle nudge. It is time for Daisy to stand. The little calf is still weak and her legs want to move in all different directions. When she finally stands, her legs are very wobbly.

Now that she is standing, Daisy wants to eat. She is hungry. She needs to drink her mother's milk to grow stronger. Daisy moves a little closer to her mother's side. Mother Cow can give milk now that Daisy has been born. Daisy finds Mother Cow's udder and begins to drink the nourishing milk.

When Daisy is a little older, the boy opens the barn door. Daisy steps into the warm spring air for the first time. She blinks her eyes at the bright sun. A dragonfly flits in front of her nose. Daisy is not sure what to make of this odd creature. She shakes her head and watches as it flies off into the sky.

Daisy hears a noise and turns to look. It's a mother pig and her babies. As Daisy walks near the fence, she sniffs the white flowers. Then she tries to reach the grass just beyond the wooden posts. She squeezes herself under the fence, but she is too big.

Daisy is hungry again. Now that she is older, she doesn't drink Mother Cow's milk. She drinks powdered milk and water. The boy brings it to her twice a day. He puts it in an oversized bottle, and she drinks out of it.

The boy loves Daisy. Each day, between chores, he comes to pet her. The boy wants to take Daisy to the county fair. He tells Daisy that she will be the best calf at the fair.

But they must work hard. There are many things for Daisy to learn. She has to learn how to stay calm around people and lots of noise.

Daisy likes to walk with the boy. But not today. She wants to stay in the barn. The boy knows it is important to practice every day. He pulls on the rope to get her to move. The boy leads Daisy out of the barnyard.

They walk to a nearby field. "Stop," he tells her, but Daisy keeps moving. She wants to look at a rabbit peeking out from a bush. The boy leans against her and pushes hard. Finally she stops.

"Now start," he calls, but Daisy wants to stay. She likes chewing on the tender grass and standing under the shady trees. The boy digs his heels into the ground. He pulls on the reins with all his might.

At the fair, Daisy needs to look her very best. Her coat must be clean and her hair cut just right. The boy takes Daisy out into the pen. It's time to practice giving her a bath. Daisy likes the cool water squirting out of the hose. She stands quietly while the boy scrubs her with a brush.

The boy dries off Daisy and steps back to admire her nice clean coat. All that's left now is Daisy's haircut. The boy brings out the clippers. Daisy stands very still while the boy trims her coat and tail.

The boy is sure that Daisy is the best-looking calf ever!

The fair is a big, colorful, noisy place. Smiling people are walking everywhere. Children ride the Ferris wheel and play games to win prizes. People eat corn on the cob and cotton candy. Others look at the prize-winning pies that people have made or the food they have grown.

Daisy is staying in a big barn where there are many calves and cows. Daisy and the boy rush to the barn so they can prepare for the big competition.

In the barn next to Daisy's barn, the pigs oink as boys and girls get ready for the competition, too. The horses neigh in the next barn. Everyone is so nervous.

Daisy moves restlessly in her stall. She can tell something is different today. Boys and girls rush all around to get their calves ready for the judging.

Daisy must look her best today. The boy brings out the combs, brushes, and shampoo. He hooks up the water hose and sets out the dryer.

First, Daisy gets a bath. Then the boy brushes Daisy until her clean coat shines brightly. Then he clips some of her hair around her head. Finally, he fluffs up the hair on Daisy's tail. Now she is ready for her new leather halter. And it is time for the competition to begin!

The boy leads Daisy into the ring. She follows the boy just as he has taught her. When he stops, she stops. When he says turn, she turns.

Daisy and the other calves line up now, nose to tail. The judges watch Daisy to see how well she minds the boy. The judges walk past the calves and look at each one carefully.

Now the calves are side by side. With the boy's help, Daisy carefully lines up her feet. They stand proudly as the judges check Daisy's ears, lift her tail, and feel her coat. Now they walk around the ring one last time. The judges decide who is the best. It's Daisy!

Daisy is back in her stall in the barn. People stop to look at the prize-winning calf. The boy talks to them and tells them how proud he is of Daisy. She is the blue-ribbon calf, they all say, just like the boy knew all along.

Baby Dolphin

Written by Sarah Toast

Illustrated by Gary Torrisi

In the warm waters near the shore, a small herd of bottlenose dolphins plays among the waves. Two leap together high into the air, then they arc and dive in. Two other dolphins ride the surf on an incoming wave.

The dolphins move their tail fins up and down to gain speed. They use their flippers to make sharp turns and quick stops.

Dolphins can swim as fast as 23 miles per hour, and they can jump ten feet into the air.

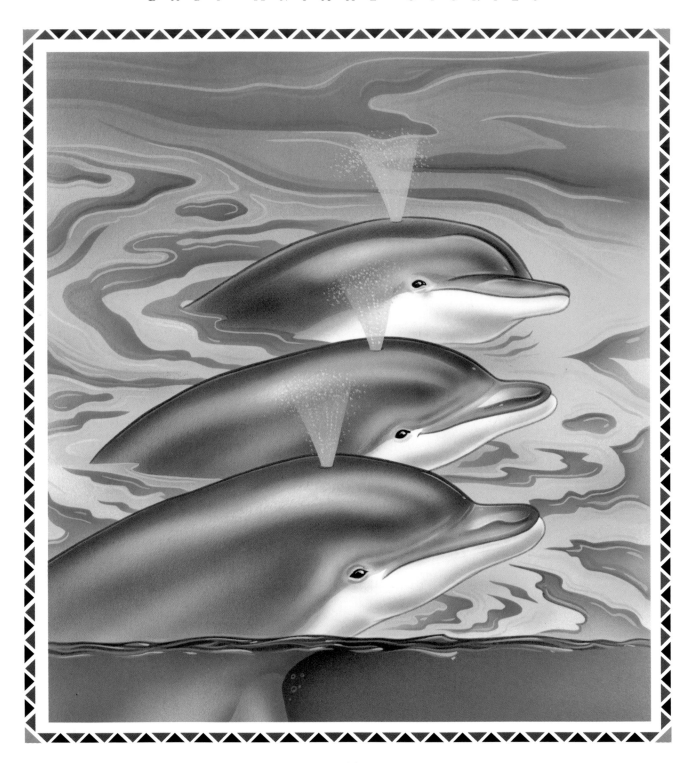

A small group of dolphins hunting for fish comes up and "blows" together. The dolphin in the front is Mother Dolphin. She must go to the surface to breathe through her blowhole.

Dolphins are mammals which means they breathe air out of blowholes on the tops of their heads. They return to the surface for air about four times each minute.

Dolphins find fish by making clicking sounds and listening to the echoes that bounce back. The dolphins can talk to each other by whistling and calling.

Mother Dolphin and two other adult dolphins find a school of small fish in the shallow water of a bay. The dolphins rush at the fish.

The fish are swept up in the wave and pushed ahead of the speeding dolphins. They land on the sandy shore. The three dolphins snap up the fish and slide back into the water.

Dolphins may look like fish, too, but they are really warm-blooded mammals. They breathe air from the surface, give birth to live young, and nurse their young with milk.

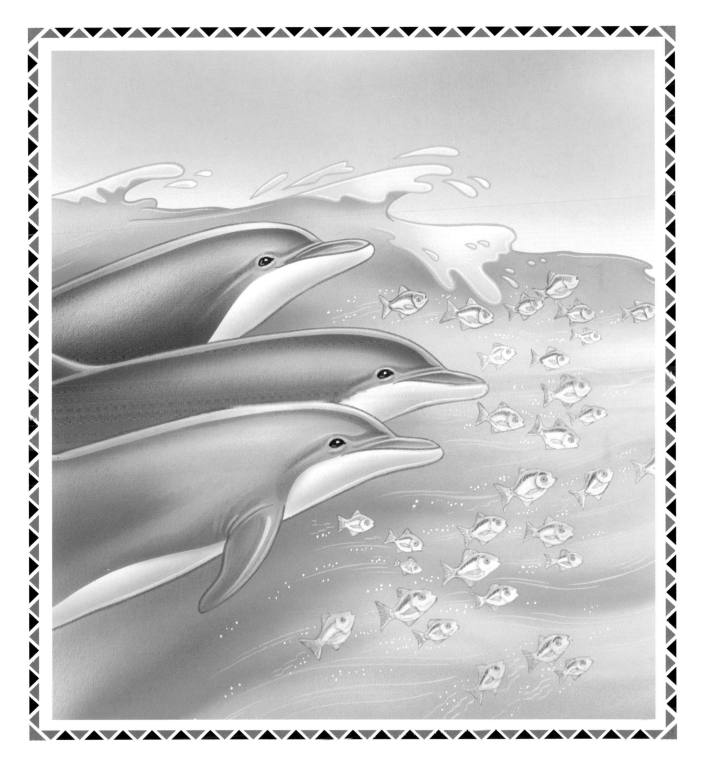

Soon Mother Dolphin will be ready to give birth to her baby. She has help from two dolphin "aunties," who stay next to her. Other dolphins from the herd gather around them and whistle softly.

As soon as Baby Dolphin is born, the two helpers guide her to the surface of the water for her very first breath. After she breathes, Baby Dolphin can float.

Dolphins have their own underwater language of sounds, clicks, and whistles. They use these sounds to communicate with each other and the environment.

Mother Dolphin nurses her hungry Baby Dolphin near the surface of the calm ocean water. Mother Dolphin floats on her side and squirts her extra-rich milk into her baby's waiting mouth.

Baby Dolphin floats near the surface so she can breathe while she is fed. The "aunties" stay nearby and encourage the mother and baby with soft sounds.

Mother Dolphin will nurse Baby Dolphin for a long time. As Baby Dolphin gets older, she will eat fish, shrimp, and squid.

Mother Dolphin stays beside her baby throughout the summer. The "aunties" also take care of Baby Dolphin.

Baby Dolphin is very playful and curious. She can swim well and loves to nudge her mother. Baby Dolphin is growing fast. Soon she will grow a thick layer of blubber like her mother. It will help her float and keep her warm.

Baby Dolphin is getting tired after playing so much. At night, she sleeps just below the surface of the water like the other dolphins.

Baby Dolphin is quick to learn each dolphin's unique whistle. The dolphins in the herd also bark, click, moan, and mew to keep in touch with one another and express their feelings.

Dolphins have no vocal chords, but they can produce sounds with a special oil-filled organ in their foreheads called the melon. These sounds come out of their blowholes.

The dolphins work together to take care of Baby Dolphin and the other young dolphins. They cooperate in feeding and defending the herd.

The dolphins are all spread out when a shark swims close to their group. Grown-up dolphins quickly surround Baby Dolphin and all the other young ones to protect them.

Dolphins always travel in small schools, or groups, to protect themselves against predators.

Suddenly four other grown dolphins rush toward the menacing shark. The adult dolphins ram it hard with their beaks, lifting it clear out of the water.

The shark flees, but some of the dolphins are exhausted and hurt. They help lift each other to the surface so they can rest and breathe through their blowholes.

The danger is gone, but Baby Dolphin stays close to the older dolphins. Baby Dolphin floats up with Mother Dolphin to take a breath of fresh air and rest for a short time.

If dolphins can protect themselves against their enemies like the shark, they can live a long time. Some dolphins live up to 35 years in the wild.

After the dolphins have rested, they celebrate by playing games in the warm water. Baby Dolphin flips through the air and uses her tail to splash her friends.

Duckling

Written by Sarah Toast

Illustrated by Judith Love

It is summer, and Mother Duck is making a nest. In a clump of reeds near the edge of the pond, Mother Duck finds a hollow place in the ground. She lines it with grass and soft cattail stems.

Mother Duck lays her nine smooth eggs. She plucks soft feathers from her breast to line the nest and protect the eggs.

Inside each egg is a tiny, growing duck. Each little duck is attached to a bag filled with thick, yellow liquid called yolk. Yolk is special food for the tiny ducks. It helps them stay healthy and grow until they are ready to hatch.

Mother Duck sits on her eggs for many days and nights. Whenever she leaves the nest, she covers her eggs with a soft blanket of down to hide them and keep them warm.

At last Mother Duck hears the "pip-pip" of her ducklings working to get out of their egg shells. The last of the little ducklings to break out of its shell is called Dabble.

Baby ducklings peck their way out of their egg shells by using a special egg tooth. This egg tooth is located on the tip of the little ducklings' beaks. The egg tooth will soon fall off, since the ducklings will no longer need it.

Mother Duck protects her new ducklings by rubbing her tummy feathers over them in the nest. Now the ducklings are waterproof. They will stay warm and dry when they swim.

Mother Duck can waterproof her own feathers by combing oil into them with her bill. The oil that she uses comes from a place near her tail.

When ducks rub this oil over their feathers, it is called preening. The oil hardens and the feathers become waxy, allowing the water to roll right off.

By keeping their feathers dry, ducks can fly as soon as they leave the water.

While the ducklings are resting in their nest, a skunk comes to the shoreline to get a drink of water. Mother Duck and the ducklings try to stay very still and quiet so the skunk will not notice they are nearby.

Mother Duck's spotted brown feathers and the stripes on her ducklings help them all blend in with the tall grasses and reeds that are near the water's edge.

In order to remain safe, the ducklings will stay very close to their mother until they learn how to fly. It usually takes about two months before most ducklings are able to fly.

Dabble is a special type of duck known as a dabbler duck. She sees Mother Duck taking good care of her brothers and sisters. She knows that her mother will take good care of her, too.

The tiny ducklings are only a few hours old, but they already are able to run. They follow their mother down to the water's edge to take part in their very first swim.

Ducklings can usually swim very soon after they are born. But they must wait for their mother to waterproof their feathers. Since Mother Duck has already taken care of that, the ducklings are ready for their first swim!

Dabble is the very first young duckling to jump into the water after Mother Duck. Her sisters and brothers gleefully jump in after her. They bob on the water like balls of fluff.

What a glorious and fun pond! Suddenly Dabble is dazzled by a dragonfly that lands on a nearby lily pad. Then a caterpillar on a cattail leaf grabs Dabble's attention.

Now Dabble is becoming quite hungry, and she knows exactly what to do. She tips up her tail and stretches her bill down to the muddy bottom of the pond, where she finds plenty of plants, roots, and seeds to munch on.

Dabble enjoys dipping down to look for food underwater, then popping up again to see all of her brothers and sisters and Mother Duck.

Dabbling is what Dabble does when she turns upside down to look for food underwater. Only her tail can be seen above the water.

Dabble watches a colorful butterfly flitting among the reeds in the pond. Then Dabble dips down to enjoy another nibble.

The pond is so much fun for Dabble! Now she lifts her tiny head to quack hello to a red-winged blackbird flying by.

That night all the ducklings sleep safe and warm in their nest after their busy first day in the world. Dabble is dreaming of tomorrow, when she will see the bright butterfly again.